THE BEE GEES

KIM STEVENS

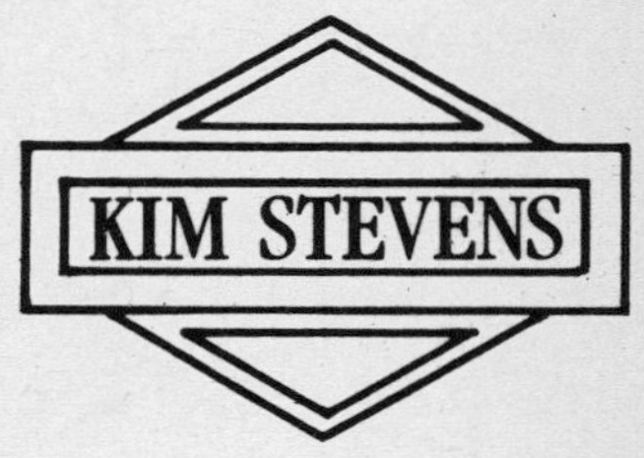

SCHOLASTIC BOOK SERVICES
New York Toronto London Auckland Sydney Tokyo

This edited edition is published by Scholastic Book Services, a division of Scholastic Magazines, Inc., 50 West 44th Street, New York, N.Y. 10036, by arrangement with Quick Fox, A Division of Music Sales Corporation.

12 11 10 9 8 7 6 5 4 3 2 1 3 9/7 0 1 2 3 4/8

Printed in the U.S.A. 01

CHAPTER ONE

There's no better tune in the world to sum up the unique story of the Bee Gees than "Stayin' Alive," the hit song from *Saturday Night Fever*. For the Bee Gees have indeed stayed alive. They've weathered social and political changes in the world as well as major changes in their own lives and music. And they have proven themselves to be musical survivors. They have stayed *alive and well*.

Who are the Bee Gees? Oddly enough, that's a matter of dispute. Oh, yes, everyone knows that the Bee Gees are the Brothers Gibb, consisting of Barry Gibb, and his fraternal twin brothers, Maurice and Robin. As a matter of fact, so phenomenal is their fame at this stage of the game, it's hard to imagine anyone *not* knowing who the Bee Gees might be.

The disagreement about who the Bee Gees are centers around their music. They have been called everything, from geniuses to Beatle clones. They've been worshipped and they've been put down. And somehow, the Bee Gees have managed always to be noticed.

The Bee Gees have always had their admirers. There are critics who can't stop raving about them. But they've always had their detractors as well, those who say the secret of the Bee Gees' success is simply that they can sound like whoever is hot at the moment.

In fact, the Bee Gees always sound like the Bee Gees, and there's definitely such a thing as "The Bee Gees sound." When a song comes on the radio, almost every fan can tell if it's the brothers singing or not. There's Robin's clear, high vibrato. There's that unmistakable three-part harmony. There's that lush romanticism, those sweeping chords and surging arrangements. It's always the Bee Gees sound all the way.

But the Bee Gees have a certain versatility that allows them to change their style in a manner other groups can't master. They can adapt their personal style to whatever's hot at the moment without losing anything. They are unique but they're also familiar. They can do folk or disco, rock or middle-of-the-road. They can even sing the Beatles' trademark tunes from *Sgt. Pepper* and leave their own brand on those songs.

The Bee Gees are very much aware of who they are and what they're able to do. "We're fully aware that our music is almost totally commercial," Barry says in answer to criticism. "We write for the present."

That they have managed to keep changing while retaining their own special sense is what makes the Bee Gees such ace survivors. They've been up and they've been down. They've been a

Neal Preston/Camera 5

tightly-knit group and they've been bitterly spilt from one another. And all the time, they've been concentrating on staying current, keeping up to date. "I think that we have really all grown older. Our music has changed . . . ."

As far as the brothers are concerned, their music has changed for the better. "We were always writing the same kind of music," Robin explains, "only we weren't putting it down right."

What is their kind of music? Barry described the current Bee Gees sound as "nuance sounds in an R & B framework."

And what did the Bee Gees sound used to be? Nuance songs without the rhythm and blues framework would be one way to describe lush ballads like "Words" and "Massachusetts" or richly orchestrated rock like "I Can't See Nobody" and "Nights on Broadway."

"If you look at our past history, it's gone from one form of music to another. We're a band that likes most kinds of music, and in five years, you may not find us doing this anymore."

"This" is the hottest disco sound in America at the present time. It's what has netted the group somewhere between $12 and $15 million on *Saturday Night Fever*—so far. And even the Bee Gees readily admit that "this" music is different from what "that" music used to be.

" In the earlier days," Robin explains, "I suppose we weren't as experimental as we are now, but one didn't have to be."

And Barry says, "We never had a good band in the past. Most of the early songs are very simple and have simple backing. We colored our songs with strings because we didn't have musicians who could add color themselves. Now that we've got that, it's helped steer us in the direction that we want to go."

The former Bee Gees sound has been summed up as "grandiose" and "overly orchestrated." It's true that the boys would often be backed up by a thirty-piece orchestra with a large string section. But even if Barry today dismisses the sentimentality and gushing strings as "outside coloring," the fans have always loved it. The old Bee Gees' tunes are a blend of pop and pathos. Listening to a song like "I Started a Joke" or "I Can't See Nobody" is like tuning in to an aural soap opera. The music sweeps and surges like a silent movie background, creating an atmosphere of broken hearts, shattered dreams, high

David Gahr

ideals. The singers' voices tremble, almost breaking, as if tears can never be far away. It's theatrical, and it's unique.

The Bee Gees' romanticism has always been thickly frosted with a wholesome innocence. Their songs have always had — and continue to have — a freshness and ingenuousness that tougher rock bands disdain. What could be more fitting in these days of Bowie and Patti Smith, of punk groups like Johnny Rotten and the Sex Pistols, or the leather-jacketed, street-smart Ramones than the overwhelming popularity of the Bee Gees? They sing about love and ambition, about dreams and frustration, with an old-fashioned straightforwardness that's hard to resist. Critics might call the Bee Gees surge a type of backlash against more "progressive" sounds, but if it's backlash, it's the nicest kind.

"We used to have a lot of message songs," Barry says simply, "but I don't think people want to hear about how bad times are these days. I think people are far more interested in dancing and enjoying themselves now. The important thing in life is you're supposed to have a ball."

The most impressive all-around accomplishment of the Bee Gees of late has been the sound track for *Saturday Night Fever*, 1977's hit movie which made John Travolta the hottest star of his generation and which put the Bee Gees firmly on top as the number one rock group. Though they didn't perform, as they did in *Sgt. Pepper's Lonely Hearts Club Band*, they didn't sing anyone else's music, either. It was a Bee Gees music fest from start to finish, with top musical stars like Yvonne Elliman and Tavares singing Bee

Frank Edwards Fotos International

Gees tunes as well as the Bee Gees themselves.

The *Saturday Night Fever* album managed to do what Rod Stewart, Shaun Cassidy, Kiss, and Linda Ronstadt couldn't accomplish. It pushed Fleetwood Mac's *Rumours* out of the Number One spot as the top album in America, a spot *Rumours* had been enjoying for thirty-three weeks.

At one point, with *Saturday Night Fever* the top LP, the Bee Gees also had five singles in *Billboard* magazine's Top Ten, three composed and sung by them, and two other Bee Gees-penned tunes sung by their younger brother Andy Gibb and their "discovery," Samantha Sang. The first single release from the sound track, "How Deep Is Your Love?" shot to the number one position even as *Saturday Night Fever* was just opening at theaters all across the country. Shortly afterward, "Stayin' Alive" hit the charts, only to be followed in short order by "Night Fever." Together with Andy Gibb's "Love Is Thicker Than Water" and Samantha Sang's "Emotion," this was an astounding accomplishment. Elliman's "If I Can't Have You" was doing well also.

All those facts, along with figures like the 200,000 *Saturday Night Fever* sound track albums that were practically *running* out of record stores every week, were impressive enough. And then, the record-buying public learned the amazing truth about the Bee Gees' songwriting ability. They had written five of the songs for the movie in a week and a half — and the exhilarating, intense "Stayin' Alive" had been composed in just two hours!

Gees are a legend? From their very beginning, as children in Australia, to the undisputed stardom they share today, the Bee Gees have proved themselves to be prolific composers, talented singers, and exceptional showmen. As a group, they have functioned together for over twenty years. As stars, they had their first big hit — "New York Mining Disaster, 1941" — when Maurice and Robin were only 17 and Barry, 19. And even at that time, they were such obvious hit-makers that Ahmet Ertegun, then the president of Atlantic Records, was willing to spend a quarter of a million dollars to obtain the U.S. recording rights of the group for the next five years.

Has it all spoiled them? Not a bit, say those close to the Bee Gees. They are devoted family men, with wives and children, while many record stars have groupies. They live near their parents. They travel with an entourage, but it's one made up of relatives, in-laws, close friends. They continually learn more about music, and about themselves, from their failures and successes, and they put everything that happens to them to good use.

More than a decade has passed since the Bee Gees first burst on the American rock scene with the first hit of one of the world's longest streams of hits. They have changed, and their music has reflected these changes and the changes in the world in general. They have borne their success with the same goodwill with which they've handled criticism. And they know there will be more of both in the future.

Happily for the Bee Gees, the kudos almost

always outweigh the barbs. Their work on *Saturday Night Fever* and *Sgt. Pepper's Lonely Hearts Club Band* has firmly established them as a rock group of spectacular talent, one that's going to be around for many years to come. From their early days in Australia to their days of superstardom in Britain to their unprecedented fame in the United States today, the Bee Gees have proved that "Stayin' Alive" can mean more than mere survival — it can mean getting better all the time!

CHAPTER TWO

The Bee Gees started singing together professionally when Barry was nine and the twins just seven. Most of the songs the kids were interested in singing were rock and roll, even though rock was in its infancy back in the mid-fifties. But the Brothers Gibb were already rock-oriented, and the compositions they were performing on stage at local movie theaters (between films) in their native Manchester were, often as not, by Bill Haley and the Comets. Haley was one of the top rockers in America at that time, and his biggest hit, "Rock Around the Clock," is today considered one of the great rock songs.

In 1958, the Gibb family emigrated to Australia. Hugh Gibb felt the land was rich with promise, and he was drawn by the chance to escape from England's harsh climate.

In Brisbane, where the Gibbs settled, the boys once again pursued a singing career, with mixed results. On the one hand, they got their own television show and a record deal. On the other,

Jay Webster

they just weren't becoming the successful band they'd dreamed of being. Later, Barry would analyze their lukewarm reception by explaining, "We were kids and kids don't buy kids' records. Now it's sex appeal. We're old enough to have kids be attracted to us."

Still, at the same time, the boys didn't realize that they'd have future sex appeal to bank on. They were only aware of one thing — after several years of struggling, they weren't making it in Australia the way they'd hoped they would.

That doesn't mean they were a failure. In March, 1960, they began their own weekly television show, a half hour on Brisbane's ABC channel. By 1963, they'd signed with Australia's Festival record label and recorded their first Bee Gees-written single, "Three Kisses of Love." But that just wasn't enough.

"We released about thirteen records in a row in Australia," Barry later reminisced with writer Jim Girard, "and they were all flops. None of them took off."

By this time, the Bee Gees were veterans of the musical scene. They were also cognizant of their own talents. The Sixties music boom was in full swing, and there was no doubt where it was all happening. It was happening back in England. It had stemmed from the cellar clubs in Liverpool, where a young musician named George Harrison stepped into a band with three other Liverpudlians. Pete Best (later replaced by Ringo Starr), John Lennon, Paul McCartney, and Harrison soared as the Beatles and made

England *the* place to be if you wanted to find fame as a rock star.

It wasn't an easy decision to make, and the Bee Gees didn't just suddenly bolt back to Great Britain. They had lived in Australia for half their lives. They felt as Australian as they did English. Besides, they felt that their adopted land was shaping their musical future. As Barry says, "Australia was good to us in that that's where we got our basic training. We worked adult clubs before we made records." And besides, perhaps being half a hit in Australia is better than flopping in London.

Eventually, the boys decided they'd be better off trying their luck back in England rather than sticking it out Down Under. Interestingly, by the time they were finally totally committed to their decision to leave, they were becoming quite successful in the land they were leaving. In early 1967, when the Bee Gees left Australia, they'd already gotten three of their songs on the Australian charts in the number one position. Also, they'd been voted the top songwriting team of both 1965 and 1966 and had been presented with a special award as Australia's best group of 1966. They weren't leaving as unknowns.

When the Bee Gees reached London, the Beatles weren't the only group to have achieved wide popularity. Heavy metal groups like Cream were right on top, along with acid rock bands like Country Joe and the Fish and Jefferson Airplane. Could there be room for the sentimentality and sumptuousness of the Bee Gees' songs?

Richard E. Aaron

The Bee Gees made their impact on the English musical scene through Robert Stigwood, the man who would promote their rise to superstardom via the sound track for *Saturday Night Fever.* The first thing the boys wanted to do after they arrived in England was make contact with Brian Epstein, the man who managed the Beatles and who was most responsible for making them the most famous group in the world at the time.

In the hopes of snagging Epstein as their manager, the Bee Gees sent tapes to his office. But it wasn't Epstein whose interest in the Bee Gees was piqued. It was Robert Stigwood.

"When we first got off the boat from Australia, Robert knew we were in town, though we didn't know it. We had this house in Hendon and the phone was ringing all day. We didn't know who it was. I eventually answered and it was his secretary, who is now in fact my wife. She said, 'He'd like to have a meeting with you. Are you interested?' And I said, 'We're interested in meeting with anyone.'

"He was a small cog then, working with Brian Epstein, looking after the Beatles' affairs, which Brian had been completely unable to cope with. When Brian died, this position gave him a vehicle to go out and form his own company. We were with Robert the day Brian died and that's when it all happened. We've been through everything together, right from that very day."

Under the tutelage of Stigwood, the Bee Gees released their first single in England just five short weeks after they'd signed their management contract. It was an instantaneous hit.

Today, that song is still a favorite of many Bee Gees fans. Its originality was notable even when it was first released. In the middle of all the acid and hard rock on the radio stations, suddenly a new sound came on, a melodramatic, tragic tale about a totally non-existent catastrophe that caught the attention of rock audiences in a way that many harder rock melodies had failed to do. "New York Mining Disaster, 1941" surged into the top fifteen with heartening alacrity. Now the Bee Gees knew for certain that they had a future in rock and roll.

In May of 1967, the Bee Gees made their British television debut. Their appearance was on *Top of the Pops,* then the most important rock exposure in all of England. When you'd made it to *Top of the Pops,* you'd made it in London. The Bee Gees were the newest "in" group now, and the boys, as well as most of the dancers in the studio audience, wore big silver and black badges that proclaimed to the world, "Be a Bee Gee Bopper!" And some days, it seemed as if practically everybody in the whole world *was*.

"New York Mining Disaster, 1941" quickly went on to become a big hit in the United States, thereby propelling the Bee Gees right into the front lines of the international rock battle. They proved that they were equal to the pressure when their first album hit the record racks.

Bee Gees First, their premiere LP, was an automatic hit, since it contained their first hit tune. It wasn't long before other songs from that album became popular hits, and, with the re-

David Gahr

lease of their second LP, *Horizontal*, their future was assured.

In their first two albums, the Bee Gees included songs that are considered classics today, songs like "Holiday," "I Gotta Get a Message To You," "I Started a Joke," "To Love Somebody," and "I Can't See Nobody."

Even then, the Bee Gees were learning to deal with the criticism they were receiving. Nothing provokes barbs like success, and the overwhelming popularity of the Bee Gees was causing many people in the rock business to get on their case.

Right from the very beginning, the Bee Gees were accused of "copying" everyone from Manfred Mann to the Beatles to Herman's Hermits. Few of their detractors ever admitted that the ability to vary their style on different songs was just an added talent of the Bee Gees. Of course, the boys never for a minute thought of themselves as carbon copies of any other group. And they weren't. They were just turning out commercial hits the way they knew best — by giving the public the kind of music it wanted to hear.

It seemed as if they couldn't win. On the one hand, they were being criticized because they were too much like everyone else. On the other, they were being jeered at for being too different. They were being put down for "corniness" and "sentimentality." Their accusers never mentioned the fact that it was their lush vocals and rich orchestration that made them sound like the Bee Gees and not like any other group.

Even if certain critics didn't like them, the record-buying public certainly did, and that was what mattered most at the time. When "I've Gotta Get a Message To You" was released in the United States in 1968, it became their first U.S. Top Ten single. And their next hit, "I Started a Joke," made it to the Top Five. In the meantime, they'd released their third album, *Idea*. They seemed firmly entrenched as a top rock group.

By this time, the Bee Gees had evolved an identity all their own. When they made their first American tour, early in 1968, the stadiums and concert halls were filled to overflowing with screaming, adoring teenagers. They were backed by a 30-piece orchestra, as they sang all the songs they'd written themselves. With 23 strings, a harp, and six horns behind them, the Bee Gees emerged sounding sweet and innocent, especially when Robin approached the microphone and sang longingly in his emotion-filled, pleading vibrato.

In 1967 and 1968, one hit followed another. "Massachusetts," "Words," "World" — it seemed as if the progressive string of Bee Gee smashes need never end. And certainly there was never a group so prolific. When "World" was released, it was with the information that Robin and Barry put it together by each writing separate versions in five minutes and then combining them, with one version becoming the chorus and the other version, the verse. Little wonder that groups who labored for weeks over the writing of just one song should feel a certain amount of resentment at the Bee Gees' swiftness and confidence.

The Bee Gees' image at this point was as cleancut as anyone could get. Their press agents informed people that they took no drugs, drank nothing alcoholic, and didn't smoke. Their second album, *Horizontal*, was described by the Bee Gees themselves as "reality against fantasy," an anti-psychedelic effort.

In addition to all this good press material, there was Maurice's marriage to the singer Lulu, which once again catapulted the Bee Gees into the limelight. Rock marriages are always a source of interest, especially if both parties are singing stars, and Lulu was a big favorite of rock fans, especially in England.

It seemed as if nothing could stop the Bee Gees now, and they even dared to turn out an unusual album called *Odessa*, their most experimental effort at that time.

Odessa was not a big hit, but many critics still consider it their most impressive, mature work. It's become a sort of underground classic, in fact.

By 1968, the Bee Gees had been together as an act for ten years. They had accomplished a great deal in that time. It was the classic success story. The Bee Gees had made it, and by the time they were considered established rock stars, Barry had just turned 21; Maurice and Robin were still in their teens. It seemed that the sky was the limit.

Even during their brief time on top, the Bee Gees had made it clear that they weren't content to sit back and rest on their laurels. They put out an astounding number of singles in a short period of time. They filled the record racks with their hit albums. They worked long hours in the studio, practicing and perfecting their vocal

United Press International

harmonies, their intricate melodies. They always wanted to grow.

And, in the ten years they'd been performing, they *had* grown. They'd gone from being three cute little kids singing in the afternoon kiddie show in Manchester to being three consummate entertainers who knew just how to give their audiences what they wanted. They knew the ropes. They knew who to trust and who to depend on. They knew what their fans wanted and exactly how to play to them.

And yet, all this time, they weren't satisfied. What they had wasn't enough. They weren't happy. Like so many other groups who weren't feeling good about themselves, they ended up doing something that shocked and upset their fans perhaps even more than it upset them. In short, just when they were on top of the rock heap, the Bee Gees called it a day. They split up.

Richard E. Aaron

CHAPTER THREE

Once, when asked why the Bee Gees were still together after so many years, Maurice Gibb grinned and revealed, "Because we're nuts." Later, he admitted that was a very joking way of expressing a very complex set of reasons. The Bee Gees aren't together today simply because they're three carefree brothers who never considered doing things any other way. They're together precisely because they did do it another way. If they hadn't broken up when they did, perhaps the Brothers Gibb *wouldn't* be together as a musical group right now.

Groups split up for many different reasons. Sometimes it's a conflict of musical direction that makes individual members want to run off in different areas. Sometimes it's the fact that a backup member wants to go it alone with his own group. Sometimes it's rivalry. Other times personal conflicts just can't be resolved.

When a group breaks up, it's often impossible for them to ever get back together. The Bee Gees,

Wide World Photos

when they list their many accomplishments over the years, can add to that impressive list the fact that they're one of the few groups in rock history who broke up, came back together, and managed to be an even bigger hit the second time around.

The breakup lasted fifteen months. It happened in 1969, and today Barry's voice still sounds stunned when he says, "It took us two years to get back together."

What made them split when they were at the peak of the mutual success for which they'd strived so hard and so long? Today, Maurice simply chalks the split up to "immaturity." But it wasn't nearly that simple.

Barry is probably closer to the point when, in discussing the breakup of the Bee Gees, he remembers, "We'd become enemies — the magic was lost." For the Bee Gees, success had proved to be the hardest medicine to swallow.

It's far from unusual for success to go to a star's head. It's an old, old story. And, in the Bee Gees' case, it wasn't merely the conflict of three fan-fed egos. Here were these three young guys, brothers, who became overnight superstars. They were adored by their fans, beseiged by their groupies, stalked and quoted by the press. At the same time, they were three talented and ambitious musicians functioning smoothly as a group. It wasn't always easy.

Both Robin and Barry were writing songs and Maurice was busy arranging them. These boys weren't just mouthing the lyrics and melodies of other writers. They had to function well and cooperate on the level of songwriters and musical interpreters as well as singers and musicians. Often, they would find it difficult to agree musically. Where once there had been only teamwork, competition crept in.

Then, one day, it was over. The brothers felt that the magic was gone. They wanted to follow their own separate paths.

Looking back, it's not the least bit surprising that the Bee Gees should have broken up for at least a little while. After all, they'd never had a chance to function as separate musical entities. It was always Maurice, Barry, and Robin, the Bee Gees, the three Brothers Gibb. None of them had the slightest idea of what he might or might not be able to do on his own. It had always been a brother act, three boys pursuing a common goal. Now they'd reached that goal. They had found a fame greater than they or their father had ever dreamed of back in Manchester, greater even than they'd hoped for after making a name for themselves in Australia. They knew what they'd done, but they were still unaware of what exactly they were able to do. What were their individual capabilities? Where did their collective talents lie? They had to find out, even if it meant the end, once and for all, to their familial closeness. They had to break up or risk detesting each other forever. And so, they split.

The next fifteen months were a period of growth and sadness. The Bee Gees had to think about the past individually, to try and understand their paths, to learn about themselves.

The sum total of the Bee Gees' efforts during the fifteen months they were on their own is nothing to boast about. Robin did a solo album, *Robin's Reign*, that was — deservedly — not a smash. Barry and Maurice held onto the Bee Gees moniker when they recorded the similarly ill-fated *Cucumber Castle*. Solo singles by Maurice and Barry also bombed out.

The boys got back together, drawn by the same force that had made them a singing group in the first place — their sense of family, their blood ties. As Robin recalls it, "If we hadn't been related, we would probably never have gotten back together."

By that time, all three brothers had cooled off, matured, gained a greater understanding of the magic that lay in their continued teamwork. "We had to get back together," Maurice says, "because the formula was between the three of us. But the image of the Bee Gee brothers had

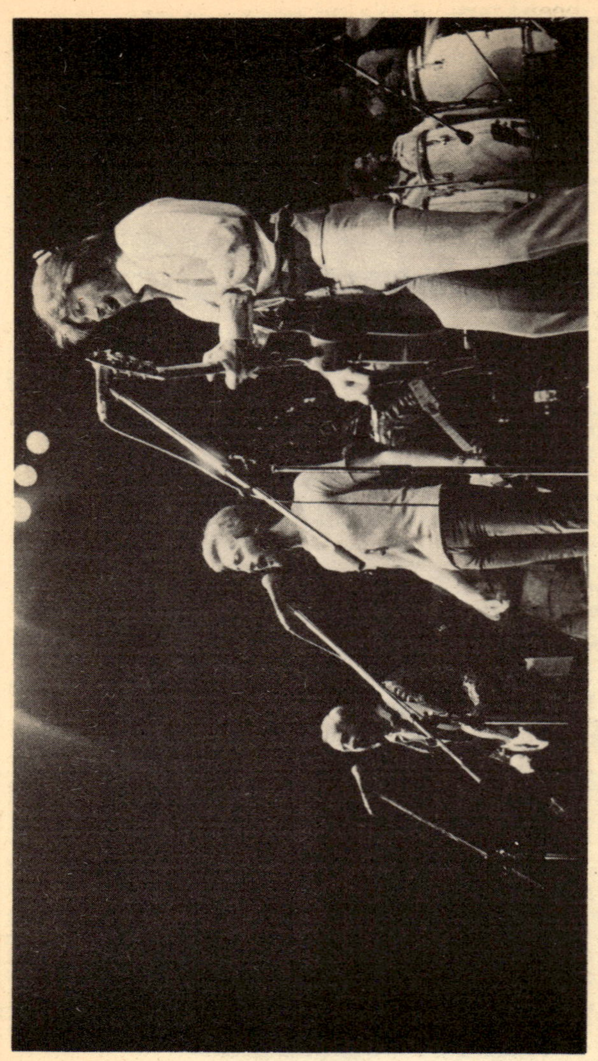

Richard E. Aaron

been smashed. We knew it would take five years to get to know each other again like we did before we started arguing."

The first thing all three Gibbs had to do was admit that splitting up had been a mistake professionally and accept the fact that they were stronger together than alone. And that's the first thing they did. "We found out we did have the same goals, so why do it separately?" is how Barry remembers the return to the fold.

They started out on a new tack. Since people had always been demanding ballads of them, the Bee Gees tried to give people softer, sweeter music. But what they were coming up with didn't make it. Their new songs were saccharine, listless. The spark which had been there in the early days was gone.

For a long time, things were looking pretty grim. Only the fact that their psyches and their personal lives were in so much better shape was keeping the band going. They came up with four albums, none of which was a winner. The songs are uneven, the choices confused. They sound like what they were — a group trying to get to know each other all over again. And the Bee Gees weren't fooled, either. They knew they were missing the boat, in spite of the fact that they'd have an occasional hit single every once in a while. So dismayed were they at the music they were turning out that they finally decided to shelve an entire fifth album shortly after recording it.

Now that they'd discovered, as Maurice says, that they "weren't cut out to be solo stars," they had to decide just where they were going.

Neal Preston/Camera 5

They'd done all right with "Lonely Days" (which was number one in the United States) and "How Can You Mend a Broken Heart," but the hits were too few and too far between for a group who'd once turned out hit after hit, smash album after smash album. Sure, their *Two Years On* LP had "Lonely Days" as its gold single, but that wasn't enough. They all knew deep down inside that they were taking the wrong track. But what the answer was, none of them could figure out for a long time.

The Bee Gees weren't in that big a hurry. They were still trying to absorb all that had happened to them, still working on getting it all back together. They weren't in a terrible situation; because of "Lonely Days," they at least weren't considered has-beens.

So they took things slowly, not pushing themselves to try new areas. When they look back today, they realize they were always capable of doing more than they were attempting. But during that delicate period, when they had just reformed and were being extremely considerate of one another and not wishing to rock the boat, the Bee Gees were playing a very conservative game, taking as few chances as possible. More than anything, they wanted their reconciliation to work.

Today, Robin can look back dispassionately and state bluntly, "We got stuck is what it was. We're writers, and writers shouldn't stay in one area. We are capable of writing in more formats and we like to do that." But back in the early Seventies, that's exactly what the Bee Gees weren't doing.

What were they doing? To some critics, they were simply serving up warmed over variations of ideas they'd done better in the Sixties.

But to the Bee Gees, they were all making great strides in the early Seventies. How so? Well, for one thing, they all now had marriages to which they were devoting a great deal of their time. Robin was wed to an English girl, once Brian Epstein's secretary. Barry was married to a former Miss Scotland, and Maurice had found happiness and stability with Yvonne, whom he married about three and a half years before. Sometimes, there are more important things than music.

All of this isn't to say that the Brothers Gibb didn't realize they were missing the boat somehow. Looking back on it, Barry sums it up succinctly when he remarks, "There were those couple of years when we weren't what you'd call current."

They weren't "current" at all. If anything, they were considered old-fashioned, a bit passé. Their random hits showed that the Bee Gees hadn't blown all their talent through several years of carousing during their split, but at the same time, their hits *were* random, very hit-and-miss. There was no doubt in anyone's mind that the Bee Gees weren't quite in the groove anymore.

For quite a while, their failure to reestablish themselves as the superstars they were in the Sixties didn't particularly bother the Bee Gees. When they decided to get back together after their year and a quarter apart, they'd realized that it was going to take a long time for things to

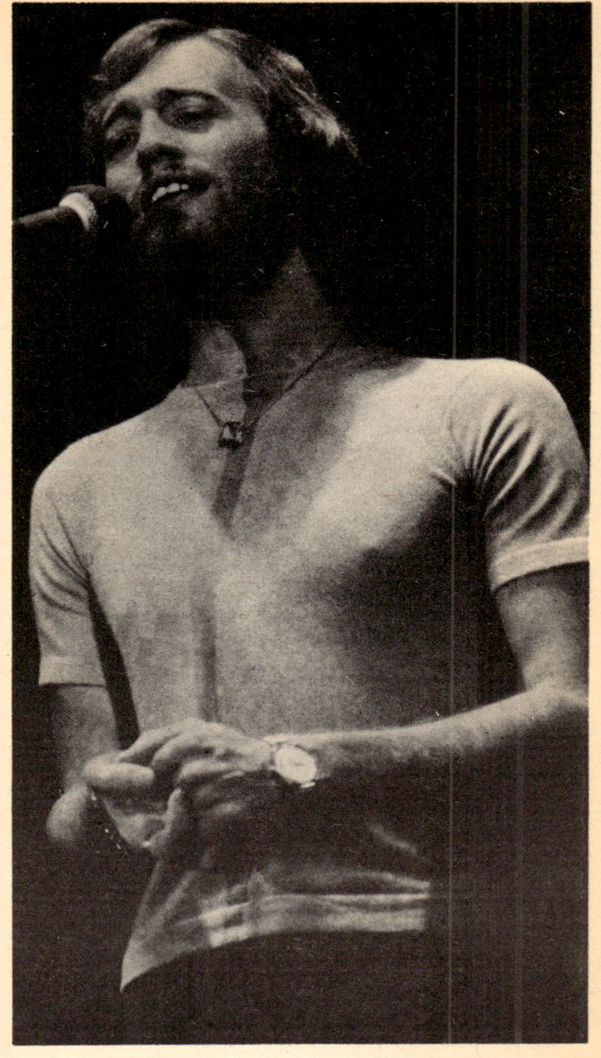

Neal Preston/Camera 5

get back on an even keel. They had been thinking in terms of five years, and, sure enough, it was almost five years before they decided to take steps toward a new kind of popularity.

And when that time came, all three Bee Gees realized they needed somebody who could add a missing ingredient, some element they hadn't managed to come up with on their own. They weren't sure what they needed, but they were smart enough to know that, after four lukewarm receptions and with a fifth album they disliked enough to shelve completely, they weren't doing something right.

And once they found their new direction, they felt sure they'd be all right.

David Gahr

The ability to knock out songs quickly had always been part and parcel of the Bee Gees, and it may, in fact, be one reason why some folks were inclined not to take them seriously. Many listeners just assume, "Well, if they wrote it that quickly, it can't be any good," without really listening to what they're hearing. As a matter of fact, one rock writer remembers a deejay raving about a record he was hearing for the first time — until he was told the group he was listening to was the Bee Gees. Then he rapidly lost interest and shrugged off the song.

Their tunes have always been written quickly, often right in the studio, where they've always made a point of having unlimited time. Since none of them reads music, they practice heavily before actually recording a song. But the song, when it's finally put on tape, might be one that they'd just written the day before — right before they started rehearsing it.

Even back in the Sixties, Maurice was telling the press candidly, "We go stale if we write a song one day and record it two days later. This afternoon we don't know what we're going to record. Otherwise you lose freshness. The song may still be good, but we're tired of it."

Getting tired of their own music is something the boys have learned to cope with. They've had to, since their concert audiences love hearing the older hits as well as the more recent ones.

Those hits have become legendary, songs like "Love So Right," "Fanny," "Run To Me," "Edge of the Universe," "Words," "Boogie Child," "You Should Be Dancing," "Lonely Days," "Nights on Broadway." Is it any wonder the Bee

CHAPTER FOUR

The Bee Gees needed something — and somebody — new, but at first they weren't sure where to start. They'd been so busy getting back into the groove with each other once again that they hadn't really kept touch with the direction in which music was going.

To make the obvious analogy, the Bee Gees were ailing musically, and what they decided to do was consult a doctor.

The man they sought out was producer Arif Mardin, a rhythm and blues specialist known as "the doctor of music." His credits at that time already included big hits with Aretha Franklin and the Average White Band. The Bee Gees were hoping he'd prove to be what they needed to get back in the swing of things once again.

Happily, they were right.

Mardin convinced them that they were right about what they'd already suspected. As Robin explains it, "You can only go on the mood of today and you can't write for tomorrow. Our trouble was we were writing in the past." Mardin was convinced that the boys had to pick up on the current, burgeoning disco sound, and he set about giving them a quick course in rhythm and blues.

The Bee Gees' first collaboration with Arif Mardin, "Mr. Natural," was released in 1974. It was a total flop, perhaps the worst they'd ever had. When you think about the Bee Gees having five of their songs in the Top Ten at once, following the release of *Saturday Night Fever*, consider the fact that "Mr. Natural" never made it past Number 178!

Still, the boys knew better than to blame Mardin for the failure. He was the first person who'd ever challenged the Bee Gees to try a contemporary soul style. They knew he was on the right track, and they were determined to stick with him.

Sticking with Mardin meant going outside themselves for inspiration. They studied various rhythm and blues stars, especially the work of Stevie Wonder. They felt right at home with R & B, even though they were aware that they'd garner a great deal of criticism for stepping into what had traditionally been considered black territory.

In spite of the fact that they knew they were going to take a lot of flack, Robin, Barry, and Maurice wanted to stick with Mardin. They felt certain that, with soul music, they'd found their groove, at least for the time being. In 1975, Barry told *Hit Parader* magazine, "We're definitely back onto an inspirational path. We know what we want to do, and we will do it. It'll take hard

David Gahr

work, but we're always collecting ideas for songs by looking around us. Everybody's dancing now and people should be able to dance to our music."

So, for the very first time, the Bee Gees had a crystal clear idea of just what they wanted their music to be. They knew Mardin was to be their salvation, and they listened carefully to his suggestions. In 1975, they enlarged the band. They added Blue Weaver on keyboards, Dennis Bryon on drums, and Alan Kendall on lead guitar. And suddenly the Bee Gees were in business as a rock band.

The result of their work with Mardin was the legendary *Main Course* album, an album filled with classics, and one that's still considered a fine example of how great a rock and roll LP can be. It was considered the Bee Gees' comeback album, and, as one anti-Bee Gee critic even ruefully admitted, the sound was "so gorgeous that I couldn't stop listening to the album." It was the Bee Gees meeting the current disco sound.

What Mardin did was to go back to using strings, but to use synthesizers as well. He invented a new kind of disco sound, a very much Bee Gees sound, blending the best of the Bee Gees' natural gifts with the hipper sound of light disco rock.

The result of all this was that there were four immediate hits on the *Main Course* LP — "Jive Talkin'," "Fanny (Be Tender with My Love)," "Nights on Broadway," and "Wind of Change." The Bee Gees were back in business — with a vengeance.

And, in answer to all those who accused the

Judi Lesta

Bee Gees of trying to cash in on the latest craze, Barry insists that this kind of music was the Bee Gees' kind of music all along. "We've always been capable of writing that kind of music," he says of the sounds that emerged from the group under Mardin's tutelage," but we were too scared of having the confidence that we could play it as good or better than others. I think the main lesson we learned from Arif was that the music has to be vibrant, it has to have some magic about it. He brought it out of us again. We knew we couldn't go in there and make another album that wasn't going to go."

So there they were, back on top. With two more hit singles — "You Should Be Dancing" and "Love So Right" — in the next year, and a well-received album, *Children of the World*, the Bee Gees had managed to recapture that old magic.

One thing that wasn't being misunderstood was the Bee Gees' phenomenal success. If they hadn't been sure that they were back on top with the release of *Main Course*, they couldn't have any doubts after they started touring. *Here at Last – The Bee Gees Live* came out of their pre-*Saturday Night Fever* tour, and it shows how they got their concert routine down pat, just like in the old days.

Here at Last is an immensely impressive album for two reasons. First of all, it shows that the Bee Gees aren't just a studio group, incapable of making good music without Moogs and echo chambers behind them. Secondly, it's a dazzling display of just how many great songs the Bee Gees had turned out in eight years. Side

One is chockful of oldies, like "I've Gotta Get a Message To You," "Love So Right," "Edge of the Universe," "Come on Over," "Can't Keep a Good Man Down," "New York Mining Disaster, 1941," "Run To Me," "World," "Holiday," " To Love Somebody," "I Can't See Nobody," "Massachusetts," "I Started a Joke," and "How Can You Mend a Broken Heart?" And if that's not enough, what about the flip side? That offers another forty-two minutes of Bee Geemania, with "You Should Be Dancing," "Boogie Child," "Down the Road," "Words," "Wind of Change," "Nights on Broadway," "Lonely Days," and "Jive Talkin'." And that's about as good an example of the Bee Gees' prodigious talents as anyone could ever hope to find. As many new Bee Gees fans don't realize — having discovered the group only since *Saturday Night Fever* — the Bee Gees have penned some of the greatest songs in rock and roll history. And their second-time-around hits are every bit as vibrant and exciting as their oldies. It's more or less true that the music of the Bee Gees can be divided into disco and pre-disco, but it's also true that both styles are still very much the Bee Gees' own, and that their own distinctive sound is present no matter what kind of songs they write and sing.

The "new" Bee Gees were immediately as popular as the "old" Bee Gees had been, and a sign of this is the fact that their *Here at Last – Bee Gees Live* album quickly sold one and a half million copies. That's really something, especially for a musical group that was considered all washed up just a few years earlier.

Bobby Bank

There's no doubt but that their plunge into what some people have facetiously termed "honky soul" put the Bee Gees back into the limelight after their years of relative obscurity. There's also no doubt about the fact that no one else has been able to do what they do better. If the accusations that the Bee Gees were no more than a copycat group were true, how is it that no one has surpassed them — beaten them at their own game — by now?

Even without the superstardom of *Saturday Night Fever*, the Bee Gees wouldn't have had reason to complain. They were successful, and they had learned a very important lesson from their breakup, a lesson that insured against the whole thing happening again. As Robin explained it, from the vantage point of his newfound maturity, "We'd only been making records for two years when the group split. We were still young, egotistical, big-headed. There was really no set musical reason for leaving."

Together again, they felt, rightfully, that they had the world on a string. Only one thing bothered them in those days before their songs catapulted John Travolta to big-screen superstardom in *Saturday Night Fever*, and that was the fact that they hadn't received the kind of recognition they felt they deserved.

As far as the Bee Gees were concerned, it was the same old story. People who oohed and aahed over what other songwriters and arrangers could do just shrugged off the multi-talented Bee Gees.

During that period of time, Robin even came right out and complained volubly about the unfairness of it all. "We put out 'Jive Talkin' when disco was very conservative. We've contributed a heck of a lot to disco. We put something else into it that people weren't doing at the time. No one gives us credit as songwriters in pop polls For instance, we get nominated in the group category, but aren't even mentioned for our songwriting. And we've written five hit songs in two years, while others picked haven't written any . . . It's aggravating."

Aggravating, yes. But it wasn't the end of the world, nor was it the worst thing that had ever happened to the group. And, at the time, none of them even suspected that the greatest success they'd yet to know was just around the corner.

Judi Lesta

CHAPTER FIVE

As soon as the movie screen lights up at the beginning of *Saturday Night Fever*, there's no doubt that this is the Bee Gees' movie as much as it's John Travolta's. Travolta's presence is certainly electrifying from the start, but he isn't the only character who shakes the theater with his intensity.

The Bee Gees are right there, from the start. As soon as the first strains of "Stayin' Alive" are heard, as soon as the film opens, it's their movie, too. The Bee Gees and *Saturday Night Fever* are inseparable, perhaps even more than the film and the actor. For instance, it's possible to imagine *Saturday Night Fever* with someone other than John Travolta playing the Tony Manero part. But *Saturday Night Fever* without the Bee Gees? That's impossible. It couldn't have been the same film without their music, so strongly did the songs define, explain, and heighten the action. The Bee Gees are the lifeblood of *Satur-*

day Night Fever. Their music sets each and every scene.

Long after people have forgotten the story line and all the actors other than John Travolta in *Saturday Night Fever*, they'll be remembering the action in terms of the Bee Gees' music. Who'll ever forget Travolta driving Karen Lynn Gorney back across the Verrazano Narrows Bridge as "How Deep Is Your Love?" floats sweetly over the sound track? Who'll forget the beautiful dancing to "More Than a Woman" or the line-dancing to "Night Fever"? The music will live on long after the film has been forgotten.

The album is, quite simply, one of the best rock and roll LPs ever. Even Rod Stewart is enthused about the album, "My absolute favorite, that first side." And Tina Turner, the queen of rock music, says the LP is " . . . good therapy for me. That whole first side sets me in a real good mood. I've worn out two or three."

There's nothing bad that can be said about the album, even though it's true that some of the material (especially on the "Night on Disco Mountain" side of the album) just isn't ever going to make it onto the charts on its own. But the fact is, the album is incredible, electric, energizing. The string of adjectives applicable to the *Saturday Night Fever* LP goes on and on.

And one of the oddest things in music history might be that, when they were trying to think of what kinds of songs to write for the film, the Bee Gees had no idea what the film was about! It's true. Many times when a sound track is written, the composer has a rough cut of the movie to

Neal Preston/Camera 5

work from. In the Bee Gees' case, they hadn't even been able to read a script before writing most of the songs for the film. "It's funny," Barry says today. "We wrote the songs for *Saturday Night Fever* without ever knowing what the movie was really about." What did they think was going to happen when the sound track was released? "None of us expected it to be so big," Maurice confesses.

While the Bee Gees may not have had a clue that they were going to have one of the hit albums of all time on their hands, others weren't necessarily so naive. The sales figures were phenomenal. As a two-record album retailing for $12.98, *Saturday Night Fever* sold with a comforting swiftness right from the start. Shortly after the film was released, the album was selling from 175,000 to 200,000 tapes and albums each day. And that's astounding!

And all that is just in the United States alone. The movie is also a smash hit in Europe, where the albums and singles were selling like bargain basement hotcakes even before *Saturday Night Fever* hit the theater screens. As they say, "When you're hot, you're hot," and the *Saturday Night Fever* sound track is about as hot as they come. It's one of the great money-making albums of all time.

Much of the album's success had to do with the film's overwhelming popularity, of course, but there's no doubt that the greatest part of the credit goes to the Bee Gees themselves. It was their reputation that pushed the album over the top. And the album was just one more example of their competence and professionalism.

Why has the sound track from *Saturday Night Fever* been such a success? Maurice suggests, "It was a combination of the two, John and us. The music made the film and the film made the music." And the music and the film combined to make many people very happy indeed. It certainly delighted John Travolta. And it's certainly kept the Bee Gees grinning — all the way to the banks and to the most secure period they've ever occupied in musical history.

Thanks to the success of *Saturday Night Fever*, the Bee Gees netted between $12 and $15 million in 1977. They're doing well enough to joke about it, as Maurice does when another statement of their enormous income arrives. "Does that mean I can keep my car?" he asks jokingly. Yes, the Bee Gees have come a long, long way.

And what has *Saturday Night Fever* meant to the Bee Gees? It's meant that they, too, have been able to develop their own production company and spend as much time as they want on their latest album. It means they'll never have another financial worry as long as they live, providing they don't just throw their money away (and that's doubtful). It means wealth and freedom and fame.

That's on the credit side, of course. On the debit side, it means that things are pretty frenzied. The Bee Gees are now acclaimed Superstars, very much with a capital "S." Their faces grace magazine covers, billboards, record jackets. Their anonymity is indeed a thing of the past.

This might sound like a wonderful treat, but

Neal Preston/Camera 5

it's not all it's made out to be, and, as veterans of success, the Bee Gees are all aware of this. The brothers are firmly committed not to allow any of the glory go to their heads. On the contrary, they're not one hundred percent pleased with all the hoopla. Sometimes they'd rather it would all just quiet down.

"It's starting to feel very much like 1967 and '68," Barry said not long ago. "It gets so everybody's running your life, or trying to, and you can't breathe. Ask our wives. If anybody knows, they do. You have to protect yourselves. Or else you end up like distant friends, passing in the corridor between appointments."

Saturday Night Fever, on the plus side, has firmly established the Bee Gees in the music industry. Finally, people talk of a "Bee Gees sound" instead of insisting that the Bee Gees' music is derivative of someone else's. At long last the Bee Gees are getting the credit they deserve as writers, arrangers, producers. Still, the fact that their sound track wasn't nominated for an Academy Award is considered a gross oversight by their fans. How could something like this happen? The general consensus is that the Academy of Motion Picture Arts and Sciences is dominated by older people, by a generation that probably didn't even sit through all of *Saturday Night Fever*. It surely seems an injustice that the music most people considered the best of 1977 was overlooked when Oscar nomination time rolled around.

The Bee Gees aren't altogether pleased with this. They cannot get over the fact that their accomplishments as writers are constantly

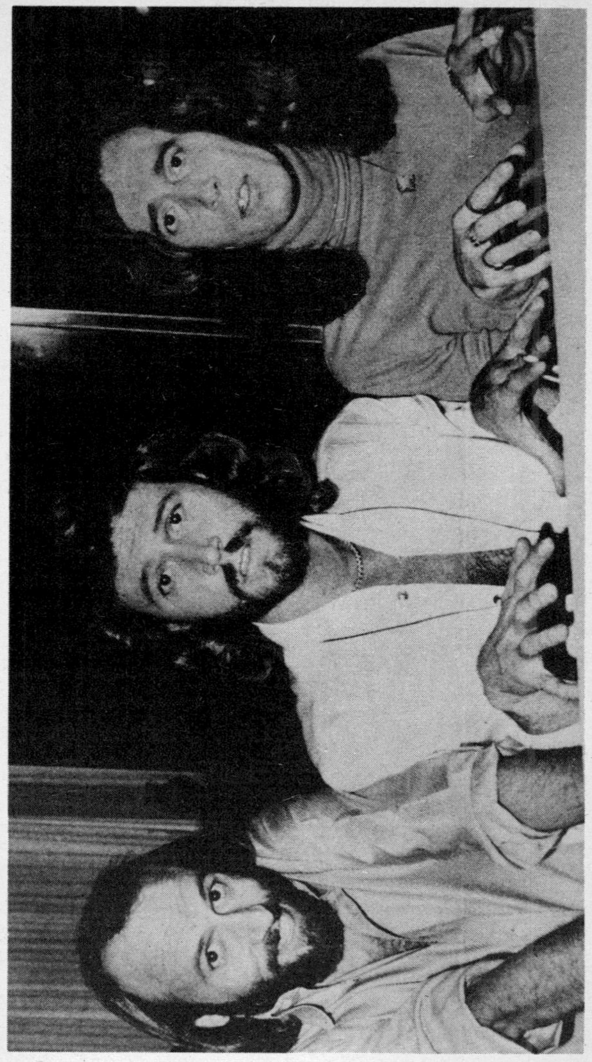

Judi Lesta

being undercut and downgraded. But at least they are able to say "I told you so" as they boost stars like Andy Gibb and Samantha Sang into the Top Ten. The "Bee Gees sound," as embodied in tunes like "Love Is Thicker Than Water" and "Emotion," is popular no matter who sings it. It's simply the most danceable, upbeat, and energetic music being played today. If the Bee Gees' music is the spirit of the Seventies, then there's some promise for the decade, after all. That seems to be the general consensus.

Even now, over a year after the movie's release, the music from *Saturday Night Fever* continues to be played. It's on the radios; it's sung on television specials; it booms over loudspeakers in discos in every corner of the world; it trembles from the lips of cabaret singers in Las Vegas showrooms. The Bee Gees' *Saturday Night Fever* album has, in short, become part of our rock heritage.

The Bee Gees once complained that they were "writing in the past." When they admitted that songwriters "can only go on the mood of today," they didn't for a moment suspect that it wouldn't be long before they were the rulers setting the mood and the pace for all the other rock bands. Once people called the Bee Gees "clones." Now the boys are having the last laugh, because don't they have more copiers than anyone else who's making records? If you want to hear how many Bee Gees clones there are today, just turn on your radios.

Saturday Night Fever has had tremendous ramifications for all those involved in it. It turned out bigger than anyone had expected,

Judi Lesta

bigger even than those who knew it was going to be a hit would have predicted.

For the Bee Gees, *Saturday Night Fever* was yet another beginning. It was *not* a "comeback" venture. The Bee Gees had long ago passed the point where they could be said to be making a comeback. If anything, *Saturday Night Fever* was for the Bee Gees a celebration movie. They were celebrating themselves and the utimate allrightness of their reconciliation in 1971 as a musical group. And they were celebrating the great shape of American music today, danceable, optimistic, and very much the Bee Gees' right to call their own.

CHAPTER SIX

These are tremendously exciting days for the Bee Gees. They have finally won the respect of other musicians. They have the financial freedom to do whatever they'd like with their private lives and their careers. And, perhaps most important of all, their private lives are very good now.

The Bee Gees are probably happier now than they've ever been. For one thing, they're old enough and mature enough to appreciate their success. And they're wise enough not to go overboard enjoying the fruits of that success.

Actually, the Bee Gees haven't allowed their *Saturday Night Fever* success to go to their heads at all. They learned enough about overnight superstardom the first time around. They've all had their flings with free spending and fast living. This time around, they're only too happy to take things slowly.

Perhaps one of the things which has meant the

most to the Bee Gees was their decision to relocate in Florida. Barry and his family live in the Sunshine State, along with Maurice and his second wife, Yvonne. Kid brother Andy Gibb, split from his Australian wife, is a Biscayne Bay resident as well. And Hugh and Barbara, the boys' devoted and doting parents, are living there as well.

More than anything, the Gibbs are involved with their families. When they were in Beverly Hills making *Sgt. Pepper*, the brothers sometimes had as many as eleven visiting relatives crammed into their rented mansion.

This sense of family has always been strong with the Gibbs. After all, it was their kinship that made them end the split that nearly destroyed their musical future. And this kinship, this blood bond, is still the most important in their worlds today. As Robert Stigwood, who's known them for such a long time, says, "They are all family people, which is very strange in this business. They don't create scandals just to see their names in print." At this point, they would all prefer avoiding scandal, by any means available. And that's not difficult, because scandalous behavior is hardly their bag anymore.

What is their bag? Working and living in close proximity to one another, enjoying the lifestyle that success has enabled them to pursue, and bringing up their children as much as possible away from the glare of the limelight.

Barry is the sex symbol of the Bee Gees onstage. Off-stage, he's very happily married and very much the family man. He's been mar-

ried for eight years to a slender, beautiful brunette named Lynda, a former Miss Scotland. They have two young children, Stephen and Ashley, and they are together constantly. Not only does Lynda often travel with Barry when the Bee Gees are on the road, she even kept him company in his trailer on the *Sgt. Pepper* set when there were lulls in the filming.

After journeying to Miami Beach on a tour in 1977, Barry decided that *this* was where he wanted to live. So he bought a big house behind gates along a private cove on Biscayne Bay in Miami Beach and then set about convincing the rest of the relatives to do the same.

Robin didn't come, although Barry thinks he's ill-advised to keep living in England and paying over 80 percent of his income to the British government in taxes. He explains, "I think we'd rather build up our incomes over the years rather than be hit the way Robin is at 83%."

Robin steadfastly refused to leave Britain for a long time. He explained his refusal to leave by saying, "I'm waiting to see what happens in the next elections. If the Conservatives get in, I'm sure they'll reduce the maximum tax rate to 50 percent."

Still, Robin, too, appears to be weakening, no matter which way England's government goes. He's been talking about moving to the States lately, with thoughts of settling on Long Island. Obviously, this Bee Gee likes his weather a bit chillier than Florida can offer. And, if he's drawn to London's cool, damp weather and a climate that's full of changes, he'll probably be much happier on the outskirts of New York than he would be living a stone's throw from the hot climes of Miami.

Robin's English estate is in the Surrey countryside not far from London. His lifestyle certainly illustrates how far the Bee Gees have strayed from the characteristic life of rock stars on the road. Robin has been happily married for years to his wife Molly, whom he met back in 1967 when he'd first arrived in London. She was working as a secretary for Brian Epstein at the time.

Robin and Molly have two children, Spencer, six, and Melissa, four, and Molly is perfectly content to stay home with the family when the Bee Gees go on tour or on a movie location. She is practically the only member of the extended Gibb family who doesn't follow the band on its travels.

In every other way as well, Robin leads what could be considered a "typical" English lifestyle. His closest friends are mostly professionals from the world of advertising and journalism. He enjoys going fishing with them in the Thames River from a boat docked at Runnymede, just outside of London.

Maurice's marital situation is just the opposite. Like Barry, he now lives in Florida. Like Barry, he takes his wife every place with him. When Maurice goes on the road, his wife, Yvonne, and their three-year-old son, Adam, are constantly by his side. That's the way he wants it.

"I *think* family," he explains. "Our mom and dad raised us that way, and her parents raised her that way."

Jay Webster

Yvonne is more than happy to stick to Maurice's side, and she likes the living in Florida as well as the rest of the family. One of the Gibbs' favorite things to do is get together and go out on Maurice's speedboat, christened "Yvonne" after his spouse. The boat is a common sight on the Miami waters, cruising along with all the Bee Gees and brother Andy soaking up the sun.

The sun is about the only thing Maurice soaks up nowadays. He's stopped drinking, completely, realizing that his alcohol consumption was the cause of many of the problems in his life. "I could stop all by myself," he says. "I did it out of family and professional responsibility. I have a clearer picture of everything now.

The sense of family is eternally strong with the Gibbs. Almost everything they do is motivated by their family feeling. Needless to say, one of the first things the boys did after moving to Florida was to get Barbara and Hugh, their parents, settled into a house of their own in Miami Beach. They never like to be separated from those they love.

The Bee Gees' wives are no exception to the rules that govern the Bee Gees. Barry's wife Lynda is now happy to have her brothers living in Florida. And Yvonne's parents and two brothers have all emigrated to Miami as well. This arrangement thrills Maurice. Rather than feel stifled by being surrounded by his in-laws, he welcomes their presence. "Her brothers play a great game of billiards," he says fondly of Yvonne's relatives, "and they look after us."

It's a family affair all the way, especially with

twenty-year-old Andy living in Florida, too. Andy skyrocketed to fame in 1976 when his single, "I Just Want To Be Your Everything," came out. It was at the top of the charts for four weeks and then turned into solid gold, leaving no doubt in anyone's mind that there was another superstar in the family.

Andy relocated to Florida after splitting from his Australian wife of 16 months. He loves the States and he's adapted to the fame that's enveloped him. So far he's developed a taste for fast cars, like the Bee Gees of old, and he bought himself a Ferrari. He's also started dating older, sophisticated women like actress Susan George, 28. One day he'll undoubtedly count himself lucky for having had three big brothers who have already been through the same trip. The sense of family extends itself to an affectionate loyalty to Andy. The other Gibbs know what he's going through, getting a taste of superstardom at such an early age. They're all there whenever he needs them for advice or direction. And big brother Barry is doing a fine job guiding Andy's career. Look at the overnight success of the Gibb-written tune, "Love Is Thicker Than Water." Through Andy, Barry has had a chance to show everyone that he's got a firm grasp of the music business and that the success of the Bee Gees was planned and not a hit-or-miss proposition.

Andy is often referred to as "the fourth Bee Gee," but he and all his brothers have made it clear from the start that he's a separate entity. He's not a Bee Gee, nor does he ever want to be one. He wants to go it alone, and he's been doing

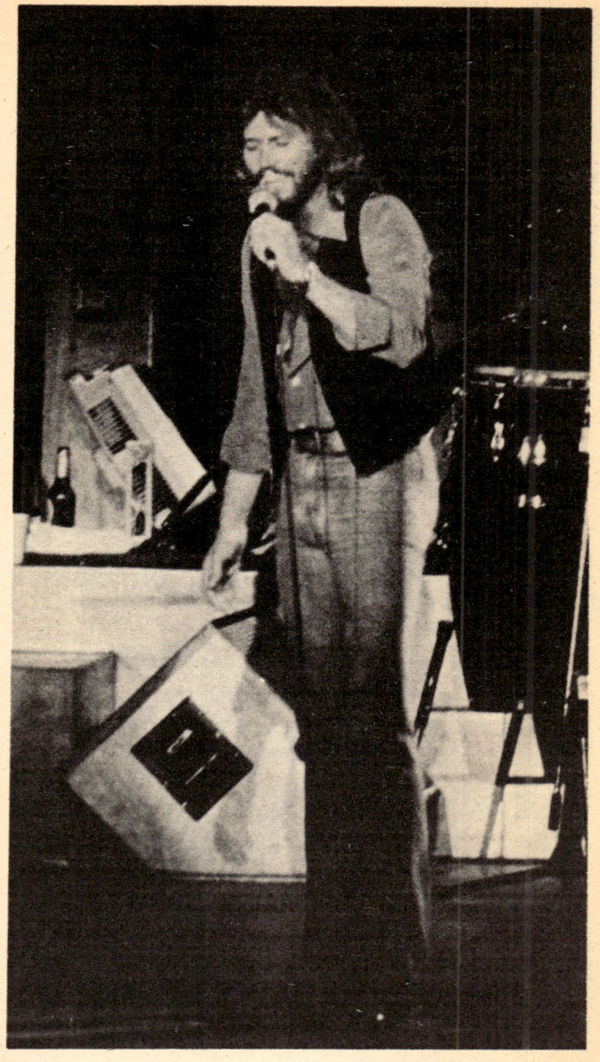

Jay Webster

extraordinarily well as a single. Since he's a decade younger than the other brothers, he manages to pick up a following that they appeal to on only a limited basis — the subteen group. Andy is currently the darling of the teen magazines. Few months go by without his picture gracing the cover of *16* or *Tiger Beat*. He's got that combination of cleancut looks and sexiness that younger girls go for. At twenty, he can still look like an innocent little kid. And his voice is as sweet and as true as his brothers' voices. He's certainly been blessed with the luck and the talent of the Brothers Gibb.

So right now, the Bee Gees couldn't be happier. They've got their mom and dad living nearby; younger brother Andy is in the fold; and Robin comes to Florida for his recording sessions even while he maintains his home in the English countryside. On top of everything else, Maurice has stopped drinking and feels that his life is finally back together again. After having cracked up so many cars in the old days, he's happier now with someone else doing the driving or when at the helm of his boat. Barry also no longer drives and is a confirmed speedboat man himself. And Robin, never one for wild living, says his main vice is drinking half a glass of vodka at night to help him sleep soundly. All of which boils down to the fact that the Bee Gees have ended up being just as cleancut now as they were back in the Sixties when they first started out. And, on top of all that, they're happier than ever.

After twenty-odd years as a brother act, the Bee Gees now have it all together, and they're

Frank Edwards Fotos International

thankful that they've emerged unscathed. They can appreciate this stage of their success, knowing that they've worked hard to get there they are, and they've tried all the different alternatives. They don't regret the period when they split and went their own separate ways. They got a lot out of that experience, even though it proved to be a painful one. Today, they all cheerfully echo the sentiments of Barry, who says complacently, "It must be a drag to be a solo artist because no one knows what it feels like except you. But the three of us can celebrate success together."

They can. And they do. They're loving every single minute of their life at the top. And who can blame them?

CHAPTER SEVEN

The Bee Gees enthusiastically feel that they're entering the best stage of their career right now, and they've got every reason in the world for feeling that way. Things are going wonderfully for the group, and they're bursting over with plans for the future. They were sent all over the U.S. during the summer of 1978 to promote their *Sgt. Pepper* appearances, and the demand for the Bee Gees as a live concert act has never been bigger.

Barry is very excited about his new career as a producer, and every Number One record by brother Andy just convinces him further that he's doing the right thing. The Bee Gees are contemplating a very happy future. "We haven't peaked yet," Robin happily predicts. "The first and second times out the Bee Gees didn't quite make it all the way to the top. This time we have. And so far, there are no signs of leveling off."

If the Bee Gees have their way, their popularity will never level off. They see whole new

Michael Putland/Retna

careers ahead of them with the success and the kudos never stopping. They're unwilling to tie themselves down to any one area. They know they can handle almost everything, and they're going to try to fit in as much as possible. That's why they turned down an offer to do a weekly television special. They don't want to get locked into anything. And, besides, the Bee Gees will remain bigger superstars if they don't become so familiar to the public that they're like the boys next door. Part of the image he's built for the Bee Gees is a private one. To their fans, the Bee Gees aren't unattainable because they're all married. They'd be set apart anyway. It's almost as if the Bee Gees aren't mere mortals. They don't give out interviews about what show they like best on the telly. They don't talk at great length about their families and their wives. They keep a low profile. In their own wholesome and cleancut way, the Bee Gees are, indeed, mysterious. And that aura of mystery is one of the things that keeps a superstar in the "super" category.

Can the Bee Gees really get even more "super" than they already are? That remains to be seen, but the prospects are more than promising. Their first venture since *Saturday Night Fever, Sgt. Pepper's Lonely Hearts Club Band,* has proved that the Bee Gees are an established box office draw. There should be more movies in the making, since the names of Robin, Barry, and Maurice on a marquee seem to be an iron-clad guarantee of any venture's success.

The boys seem headed for a movie career. Or perhaps one should say movie *careers*, as this isn't necessarily a road they would follow together. Robin was particularly blasé during the filming of *Sgt. Pepper.* He's also the one the other Bee Gees consider a born actor. He's a natural entertainer, and likely as not, it's Robin who's trying to crack up the reporter during interviews or mugging for the camera at numerous photo sessions.

While others who'd never really "acted" before might have been nervous wrecks about making their starring debut in a movie on the scale of *Sgt. Pepper*, Robin didn't bat an eye. He just took it all in stride. "I'm not particularly worried about it," he said shortly after filming had begun. "It's great fun to make a movie and there's no tension at all while you're actually doing it. That's because everything on a movie set happens so slowly there's plenty of time to think about what you're doing and relax."

The Bee Gees are pleased as punch to be starring with Peter Frampton in the movie, even though it means singing 30 songs written by another group. "What group wouldn't be thrilled to sing those songs?" Barry asks, a touch of hero-worship still present in his words.

How did *Sgt. Pepper's Lonely Hearts Club Band* go from being just a record album to being a $12 million movie musical produced by the Robert Stigwood Organization and starring not only the Bee Gees and Peter Frampton but also Sandy Farina; Steve Martin; George Burns; Allice Cooper; Paul ("Heaven on the Seventh Floor") Nicholas; Donald Pleasance; Earth, Wind and Fire; and English comic Frankie Howerd?

It all goes to show that once Robert Stigwood makes up his mind to do something, there's no stopping him. His interest in turning the LP into an extravaganza started back in 1975, when he produced *Sgt. Pepper* as a stage play. As he sat in the audience and watched all the viewers eagerly singing their favorite Beatles songs along with the actors up on stage, Stigwood realized what a blockbuster *Sgt. Pepper* could be — as a movie, not as a play. And that was the beginning of a snowball that got bigger and bigger.

After almost a year of negotiating with the Beatles (who own a piece of the movie), Stigwood got what he wanted: their signatures on a contract allowing him motion picture rights to the songs he had used on stage. The next thing was to line up a writer, a director, a musical

Judi Lesta

director, and some stars. Luckily for all of us, the Bee Gees were already part of Stigwood's stable, so it was only natural he'd ask them to be in the movie. For the leading role in the movie, he called on Peter Frampton.

Frampton is another die-hard Beatles fan. He remembers clearly the first time he ever heard the *Sgt. Pepper* album, back in England as a teenager. "There's a place in England called "Petticoat Lane," he remembers, "and . . . they always used to get the heavy albums like a week before. So I went down there and got it, and I went back home. I didn't come out of my room for about three days. I just played it nonstop . . . . *Sgt. Pepper* was the best thing I'd ever heard in my life."

But how *did* one go about making a Beatles movie minus the Beatles? That was the question. Edwards answered it by starting practically from scratch. The tunes from *Sgt. Pepper's Lonely Hearts Club Band* were used as a jumping off point, as the raw material of a film that is sheer invention. Songs from other Beatles albums are included along with all the standards from the original *Sgt. Pepper's Lonely Hearts Club Band.*

The film script undoubtedly has little, if anything, to do with what was on the Beatles' minds when they wrote the songs for the record. The film begins with a prologue in which Sergeant Pepper is marching through Germany during World War I. He has a band, fittingly yclept the Lonely Hearts Club Band. And it's this band that is knocking out the Germans. How so? It turns out that the musical instruments are magical.

Judi Lesta

When played they have the ability to fill people with the spirit of friendship. Through the goodwill the band spreads, the war is won.

After the war, the instruments are taken back to Heartland, a halcyon hamlet peopled by happy folk. For 50 years, everything is heavenly in Heartland, the trouble and unhappiness of the rest of the world never entering that joy-filled town.

This is the point where our contemporary rock idols come in. Frampton plays Billy Shears (remember him from the original title tune?), who is Pepper's grandson. Billy decides to start his own band, with the Henderson Brothers, his childhood chums. The brothers Henderson are in this case the Brothers Gibb. And, for those of you who haven't seen the movie yet, these are definitely the good guys. Actually things are so black-and-white (though always in the most appealing of ice-cream colors) in this movie that no one could ever have trouble separating the good guys from the baddies.

The love interest in the movie is Sandy Farina. She plays Strawberry Fields, Billy's girl friend. In search of musical success, Billy and the Hendersons leave Heartland to go to Los Angeles, where Billy does succeed. He becomes a rock superstar.

Enter the baddies. The villains in this case are Mean Mr. Mustard (Frankie Howerd), Maxwell Edison (comic Steve "Happy Feet" Martin), and Father Sun (Alice Cooper). They're aided by a gang of Future Villains, played by Aerosmith.

While the villains are in the process of taking over Heartland, Billy and his band are having a

Judi Lesta

whirlwind success in smoggy, rotten L.A., where they've been promoted and pushed by B.D. Brockhurst (Donald Pleasance) of Big Deal Productions.

When they hear that the evil villains are stealing the magical instruments and plundering Heartland, Billy and his band rush back to Heartland to save the town. They manage to defeat the bad guys, in an all-out battle on a pile of money, but Billy gets no pleasure from it, because in the fray, Strawberry Fields is killed.

But there's no room for an unhappy ending in Heartland or in this movie. As he's ready to attempt suicide, Billy is rescued by the weather vane on top of City Hall (which comes to life in the form of Billy Preston) and Strawberry Fields miraculously comes to life again. Yes, it's sugar and spice all the way, especially at the end, when all the Heartland residents sing their new version of "Sgt. Pepper's Lonely Hearts Club Band" aided by such special guests as Helen Reddy, Wilson Pickett, Wolfman Jack, Carol Channing, Tina Turner, Rick Derringer, the Doobie Brothers, Minnie Ripperton, Yvonne Elliman, Doctor John, Jim Dandy Mangrum, Gwen Verdon, and Keith Carradine.

How did Stigwood get such an impressive roster of guest stars? He simply invited 400 celebrities from all over the world to a special party on the set. He sent each invitee a first-class plane ticket and booked them at the hotels of their own choice. Cost of the day? A mere $500,000.

The movie is all singing, with new material written to keep the plot moving along. The only

Judi Lesta

person with spoken dialogue throughout the film is George Burns. Burns didn't have a song when the film was originally written, just a speaking part. So the eighty-year-old comic asked for one. And he was given one of his favorites, "Fixing a Hole."

The Bee Gees sing many of the songs in the film, which they all say was an interesting experience for them. Of course, the movie was made before anyone knew what a smash the *Saturday Night Fever* album was going to be, so the Bee Gees aren't really the big stars of the film. That's why some observers say the Bee Gees might not have done it the way they did if they'd know just how big their *Saturday Night Fever* fame was going to be. And Robin did sound a little disgruntled when he told a reporter, "The whole focus of the movie is on Peter (Frampton). We're always running around saving him from something."

Still, no one could say the Bee Gees complained of their roles in *Sgt. Pepper*. If anything, they were all enthusiastic about movie work. "George Burns has the hard part," Barry admitted magnanimously, "having to read the lines. I'll admit that when you have to give expressions to make each scene happen, it can be difficult, but it's always a lot of fun."

Mostly the Bee Gees had to keep telling people over and over that they don't really mind doing other people's songs, especially songs by the Beatles. "We write our own music, and we love doing it, and that's great," explains Barry patiently. "But this is a historic album being made into a film, and we're proud to sing the

Judi Lesta

music. I don't know anyone who doesn't like singing Beatles songs. It comes from a basic instinct that you enjoy singing the songs anyway. In fact, we couldn't wait to get into the studio . . . to work with George Martin, are you kidding? You just want to do that whether you're being paid for it or not."

Barry admits that George Martin, out of his innate respect for the work of the Beatles, held the Bee Gees closely in check during the recording sessions. Other than "updating" the rhythms, Martin remained true to the original musical scores, and the result was that the Bee Gees didn't always have the freedom they're used to, but they didn't really mind.

"We could have gone crazy on a lot of those tracks," is how Barry puts it. "We wanted to use falsettos and so on, and to some extent he let us do that. But not all the way. He's got real tight lines the way he wants to go, and he made that clear to everyone when we were doing it."

The result, naturally, is just what Martin was aiming for. The score, while obviously being sung by new people instead of the Beatles, is still very much the Beatles' own music. In a new framework, the story of Billy Shears and Heartland, the old Beatles music is presented in a manner that simply serves to remind everyone how far ahead of their time the Beatles really were.

It's interesting to note that the Bee Gees don't actually know the Beatles. Or, rather, they didn't know them when they were making the movie. But the important thing wasn't the Beatles themselves but the music of the Beatles. And

Michael Putland/Retna

that music was of great importance to everyone on the Heartland set.

The set itself figured as one of the stars, since it was one of the most elaborate sets ever constructed for a motion picture. Heartland was built for an estimated $1 million. It is, in effect, a real hometown setup on a back lot in Culver City, California. The most famous prop of all is the 25-foot styrofoam hamburger (complete with sesame seed bun) that dominates the town square, the infamous "Mustard Burger."

Few movies were ever as greatly publicized before their release as was *Sgt. Pepper's Lonely Hearts Club Band.* Every rock magazine in the nation spotlighted the movie. Suddenly, full color photographs of Peter Frampton and the Bee Gees, wearing bright Crayola-colored satin marching band suits or the white and gold outfits they strut their stuff in for the finale, were everywhere. Photos of the grand finale scene also abounded, with all those extra stars singing and dancing behind the Bee Gees just like the old *Sgt. Pepper's Lonely Hearts Club Band* album cover. That cover, with the Beatles flanked by a host of famous celebrities, living and dead, is legendary. Stigwood's picture, with the Bee Gees backed by a bevy of present day stars (all living and in the flesh) is destined to become a classic in its own time. *Circus* magazine even held a contest for their readers, with whoever could guess all the rock stars in the picture of the finale winning the grand prize. *Sgt. Pepper's Lonely Hearts Club Band* may be a big ball of hoopla, but hoopla and hokum can go a long way even in these jaded times.

Judi Lesta

Nowadays the need for make-believe is just as strong, if not more so. Reality in the Seventies is pretty harsh, and the violent, gritty movies flashing across the big screens are often more than anyone wants to face after a rough day of coping with the unpleasant nitty-gritty of city streets, depressing newspaper headlines, and worldwide catastrophes. In this day and age, a little bit of fluff like *Sgt. Pepper* goes a long way.

It's hard for many dyed-in-the-wool Beatles fans to imagine, but some of the Bee Gees fans who flocked to see their idols and Peter Frampton as the Hendersons and Billy Shears are too young to even remember the release of *Sgt. Pepper's Lonely Hearts Club Band* back in 1967. Teenagers today were just six and seven years old back then, and many of them are just discovering the magical world of the Beatles' greatest album through watching it all on the big screen. So the Beatles are profiting from the film exposure as much as everyone else is. Not only are they making money from it, they're also gaining new fans. 1977's surge of reinterest in the Beatles as a group and in a possible Beatles reunion continues to peak. There has even been a reissue of Hunter Davies' 1968 biography of the boys from Liverpool, revised to bring the lives of John, Paul, George, and Ringo up to date.

It's easy to say that the Bee Gees wouldn't have done *Sgt. Pepper* in a supporting capacity to Peter Frampton if they'd known how *Saturday Night Fever* was going to catapult them over the top of rock superstardom, but it's not necessarily so. The Bee Gees agreed to do something few singer-songwriters ever would have done in

Frank Edwards Fotos International

the first place — to sing somebody else's songs. That proves that their egos are strong enough not to be threatened by supporting someone else in the main role. And, of course, the challenge of *Sgt. Pepper's Lonely Hearts Club Band* was hard to resist — to be able to take the greatest music of the Beatles and in some way make it their own.

Everyone concerned enjoyed working on the movie, and everyone knows it's been a career boost for each entertainer involved. Peter Frampton was especially pleased with being able to do the film (even though he was rather displeased that he wasn't allowed to do his own stunts) and with the role he defines as "the super-white, angelic hero."

Frampton's future plans when the movie was completed weren't much different from any of the other principals. He was leaving for a three-month vacation after wrapping up the project. Then he said he wanted " to relax, write a film score, and star in more films." With his impressive screen debut in *Sgt. Pepper*, there's little doubt that he'll have the chance to fulfill all three of his wishes. Movie stardom does have a way of opening doors.

And being involved with the Bee Gees seems a surefire way for anyone's career to get a big boost, not that Frampton's particularly needed an assist. Still, the Bee Gees seem able to sprinkle their gold dust on everyone who comes in contact with them.

The magic of *Saturday Night Fever*. The magic of *Sgt. Pepper's Lonely Hearts Club Band*.

Such different movies. Such different moods. But both guaranteed of success from the start, thanks in large part to the participation of one of the greatest rock groups in the world. The Bee Gees, of course.

CHAPTER EIGHT

What's ahead for the Bee Gees? It's safe to say that the sky's the limit. They have their choice of offers to choose from, and with their own active production company to guide their careers, they'll be able to call the shots. And, happily, they've got Robert Stigwood to help hold the reins of their career, a man who's proved time and again that he knows what's best for the Bee Gees and that he knows what the public wants.

They've got more than their usual share of fans, and their popularity is now truly international. Not long ago Maurice reeled off a list of invitations and offers the band has received. "We've been asked to South America six times," he reported. "We've got a great market there, but it never comes off because the promoters can't be trusted. And here we just got a Venezuelan Gold Disc for, *Los Mejores de los Bee Gees (The Best of the Bee Gees)*. We were invited to play the Kremlin Opera House in front of all the Kosygins. And Steven Ford asked us to the

White House . . . Of course, he won't be there now."

Steven Ford might not be at the White House now, but the Capitol is not necessarily out of bounds for the Brothers Gibb. After all, Amy Carter is at just the right age to add the Bee Gees to her list of favorites (currently headed by Shaun Cassidy), and the President himself likes to keep up to date on modern music. The Bee Gees are so likeable that a weakness for their music seems to be a universal taste.

At this stage of their mutual careers, they'll undoubtedly want to concentrate on what they do best, the cleancut disco sound that some refer to as "blue-eyed disco." This is definitely the kind of music audiences enjoy hearing from the Bee Gees. Since everyone knows how prolific they are, and how they don't seem to be able to turn out an album without at least two or three surefire hits on it, one can safely predict that the next few Bee Gee albums will be eagerly awaited and will blast right to the top of the charts.

The Bee Gees enjoy being more and more "experimental" with their songwriting, and more versatility can always be expected to pour out of the recording studio in Florida. Writing new songs and trying new musical formulas seems to be the Bee Gees' own personal formula for keeping the blues away.

With Robin tentatively considering resettling in the States (and at this time, the tax situation in Great Britain shows little sign of easing), it seems probable that soon all the Gibbs will be together in America, touring, recording, and working their way into being one of the best-

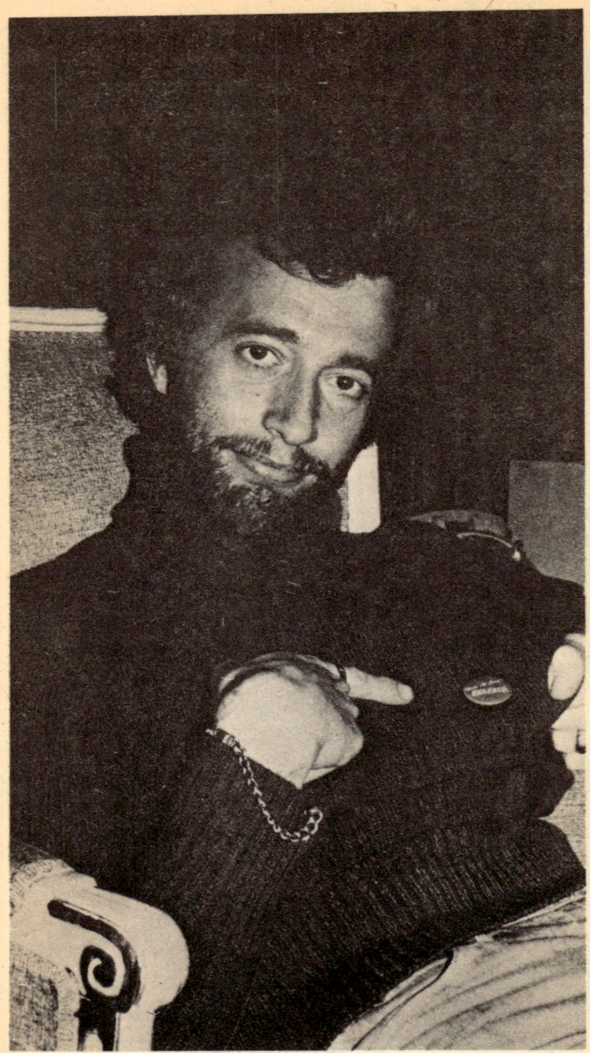

Bobby Bank

functioning financial conglomerates around.

The producing bug that has bitten Barry also holds an attraction for his brothers. It's likely that soon all the Bee Gees will be involved in production efforts, with a whole stable of Bee Gee-based stars to their credit.

Brother Andy is in the forefront of the Bee Gee followers. He has the natural charisma and good looks that are helping to make him one of the most popular young singers around; and his songs, with their infectious goodwill and unoffensiveness, are the kind of easy listening music that appeals to everyone.

Andy wants to remain very much himself, and there's nothing he hates more than being referred to as the "fourth Bee Gee." He's also vastly appreciative of what his brothers have done to help establish him as a star. "Let's face it," he says. "The Bee Gees got me started, and I owe my success to them. But now I want to record something that sounds entirely like *me*. I'm lucky enough to have three older brothers who are willing to go all the way to help me achieve this."

The hard work of his brothers in promoting his fame is typical of the Gibb family. It's impossible to imagine the Bee Gees ever splitting up again. Their sense of kinship, the blood ties of familial obligation and caring, seem to have triumphed. For the Bee Gees, their family life is the most important thing, their relationships — with their wives, children, parents and each other — the axis upon which their lives revolve. Their loyalty to each other and to their families is touching to their fans, to the point where they haven't lost any of their following despite the fact that they're all married. Though the Bee Gees are, on one level of their appeal, teen idols, none of their teenaged fans are put off by the fact that the Bee Gees all truly love their wives and refuse to hide their marriages as some rock stars do. Instead, everyone has an appreciation of the old-fashioned values the Bee Gees hold dear. The rebelliousness of the Sixties has calmed down into the new conservatism of the Seventies, and marriage and family life are again considered worthy of respect. If the Bee Gees can be called "goody-goody" as so many critics do call them, then their popularity indicated the resurgence of "goody-goodiness" as something to aspire to.

They admit they've been through it all. Their image is that they've emerged unscathed. The Bee Gees got through the Sixties with the rediscovery of old values, and so, in a way, has the world.

There's something very special about the Bee Gees, maybe because just about everyone under 35 grew up with them. Between 1967 and 1978, they've amassed a collection of hits such as the world has rarely known. Their songs have covered all the bases. In fact, listening to the Bee Gees' songs in chronological order is like listening to the history of rock and roll from the late Sixties onward.

The Bee Gees credit their "natural harmony" for much of their success, and the truth is, sweeter harmony is hard to find, if it's even possible among three singers who aren't related. Much of their success is due to their refusal to

Judi Lesta

give in, to become complacent, to settle for the easy way. They have always been willing to put themselves on the line in order to find the best sound for their abilities. Even though they write their songs in from ten to fifteen minutes, the Bee Gees are perfectionists. They've come a long way for three guys who can't read music, and the reason for this is their insistence that they always do their best work. They are never sloppy, never slovenly. They might write a song in the studio, but as soon as they've done that, they won't stop practicing it until they get it right.

Their open-mindedness has also helped the Bee Gees over the years. They listen to the suggestions of advisors, and they take any words of advice to heart. They allowed Arif Mardin to guide them in a new direction and shape their careers in a way which could have been disastrous but which, instead, brought them lasting fame. They were more than happy to make their *Saturday Night Fever* songs "more disco" in order to please Robert Stigwood. They didn't even mind cutting out the falsettos and sticking to the original Beatles scores for *Sgt. Pepper's Lonely Hearts Club Band* when they realized that George Martin wanted to be scrupulously true to the original songs. They are willing to bend, to adapt. Their ease and versatility have made them the top musical group around today.

It can honestly be said that in the world of contemporary music, the Bee Gees have no peers. Their sound was, is, and always will be, unique. Their melodic arrangements and rich harmonies have never been successfully copied by anyone else, and the lush instrumentation and careful orchestration is recognizable even to the untrained ear. Once a listener has heard a Bee Gees song, he'll never ask, "Who's that singing?" again. The Bee Gees touch is unmistakable.

Survival counts in the music business just as it does anywhere else. The respected musicians are the ones who manage to stick around year after year collecting one gold record after another, not the ones who make a big splash and then fade into obscurity. The Bee Gees have been professionals since the late Fifties, before many of their most ardent fans were even born. They've gone through ups and downs, through hits and misses, and they have managed to come through. When it comes to "stayin' alive," the Bee Gees have a lesson for everyone.

It's impossible for anyone to imagine what would have happened to the group after their breakup if they hadn't managed to swallow their collective pride, resolve their difficulties, and start putting out records again. After all, the bulk of the Bee Gees' hit collection was written *after* their initial success in the Sixties. Everyone can be thankful that the Bee Gees' ties to one another were strong enough to eventually help them overcome their differences. If they hadn't, the Seventies would have had a lot fewer hits to contend with.

We're now in a period of Bee Geemania. Everyone who's anyone seems to be singing the Bee Gees' tunes. The radios spew forth Bee Gees music at all hours of the day and night. Bee Gees songs purr from the speakers at theaters and drive-ins all across the United States and Europe. The Bee Gees' smiling faces gaze out from the covers of magazines, record albums, posters, and motion picture ads. It's a Bee Gees blitzkrieg, and no one is immune to it. People who'd never even heard of the Bee Gees a few years ago can now identify them as Barry, Robin, and Maurice. They are a living legend.

It's typical of the power of the media that a movie could make a rock group the hottest thing in the universe. And that's exactly what *Saturday Night Fever* did for the Bee Gees. It captures the heart and soul of a Seventies Saturday night. The Brothers Gibb took the aimlessness and idealism of the American teenager and wrote a Valentine to it. They elevated the commonplace into a glittering dream whose magic touched the hearts of all who heard the music. *Saturday Night Fever,* the score for which the Bee Gees wrote without ever reading the screenplay or knowing what the film was actually about, will be long remembered for its music. And it in no way denigrates the musical contributions of the others involved to say that the Bee Gees' music is probably the best of the lot.

The Bee Gees are now firmly established as one of our top pop groups, thanks to *Main Course, Saturday Night Fever,* and *Sgt. Pepper's Lonely Hearts Club Band.* Whatever hopes the former ferryboat bandleader in Manchester might have cherished about his sons' careers in music, they are all more than answered now. Hugh and Barbara Gibb are living comfortably in Florida with the rest of the family, and their

Wide World Photos

fondest dreams have come true. Nothing could please any parents more than to watch their children become major celebrities, except to see them being fulfilled in their personal lives. And Hugh and Barbara Gibb have watched three of their sons, the Bee Gees, achieve public fame and personal happiness.

Now, when Hugh Gibb watches his sons perform, it's only in the largest amphitheaters and auditoriums or on the sound stages of huge movie studios or in the air-conditioned coolness of a recording studio. The days when they sang between matinee shows as the Rattlesnakes are long gone.

Today the Bee Gees are on top and no one ever summed up things better than they themselves did when they insisted that "you can only go on the mood of today and you can't write for tomorrow . . . ." The Bee Gees have come to epitomize the mood of today. There's no other music that sums up the energy, the fear, the hopes, the newfound romanticism of the Seventies the way theirs does. The Bee Gees have always managed to capture the pulse of modern times. When it was time for message songs, they provided message, even if some of those "messages" seemed geared more toward commercialism than toward reality (like "Wind of Change," which some critics regarded as a somewhat shameless bid for the black record-buying public). When it was time for overripe sentimentality, the Bee Gees crooned and wailed with songs like "I Can't See Nobody." And when it was time for messageless rock and roll, they let loose with "Nights on Broadway" and "Jive Talkin'." Their tapping into the consciousness of the Seventies' teenager with songs like "Stayin' Alive" and "How Deep Is Your Love?" is just par for the Bee Gees' sense of what's right to sing at the right time.

For this talent, this ability to give the musical public what it wants, the Bee Gees have been praised, and deservedly so. But they've also had to put up with the criticism and abuse in regard to their versatility. They've been accused time and again of being no more than musical copycats, musicians who fashion their songs and their stylings after whoever happens to be popular at the moment. Recently, this kind of adverse criticism has died down. After having been compared to other groups ever since the Sixties, when they were being accused of aping the Beatles, the Bee Gees have at last come into their own. *Saturday Night Fever*'s fabulous roster of Bee Gees' songs was enough to shock the public and the professionals into an instant recognition of how incredibly unique the Bee Gees really are, and how innovative they have always been. And, after finally winning praise for their originality, the Bee Gees had the strength to show that they weren't afraid to do anyone else's music — certainly not the Beatles' — by appearing with Peter Frampton in the film version of *Sgt. Pepper's Lonely Hearts Club Band*, singing songs by the Fab Four from that album and others.

Yes, it would appear that there's no stopping the Bee Gees. Today, the most respectable, admired performers rave about them and sing their songs. Their names are on everyone's lips. With gold singles, platinum albums, sound tracks, and a movie appearance behind them, it seems that the sky's the limit. Doubtless, Robin Gibb is right when he insists that the Bee Gees haven't peaked yet.

Perhaps the most important thing the Bee Gees ever did was fight and break up. Their experiences as solo acts taught them how right they were together and how the magic was lost when they each tried to star alone. After months of being "miserable," they were all ready to attempt a trio again in a calmer, more cooperative manner when Robin finally picked up the phone one day and suggested a reconciliation in the studio. From that agreement to work together again came the hit single "Lonely Days." But the Bee Gees still had a few years of paying their dues to put in before Arif Mardin would help them emerge on top again with the classic album, *Main Course*. But the important turning point came when they all realized that, in Maurice's words, they just "weren't cut out to be solo stars."

Now the Bee Gees pursue the same goals. And they also pursue the same quiet lifestyles. The days when they raised Cain and cracked up a whole series of cars are far behind them. Maurice's broken marriage to Lulu is a thing of the past. He, with Yvonne, and the other Bee Gees, with their wives, have found the kind of calm contentment that only comes with wisdom and experience. They learned from their pleasures and their problems, and all three have put their lessons to good use.

There are other rock groups that could be said

Jay Webster

to be more talented in this direction or that than the Bee Gees. Certainly they lack the raw energy of Rod Stewart's band or the musical daring of the Rolling Stones. On stage, they aren't as loose as Wings or as bizarre as Kiss. They lack the overt sexiness of Aerosmith or the overt non-sexiness of Shaun Cassidy. But they don't lack any of the attributes that make them the Bee Gees and that make them a very original band in a field of imitators.

In the final accounting, the Bee Gees will be remembered most for what was so undeniably always theirs. The arpeggios, the sweeping orchestrations, the actorish posturings, the trembling vibratos, the crystal clear falsettos, the sweet harmonies, the pleading lyrics, the string sections, the meticulous melodies — this is the stuff that makes up the Bee Gees' unique contribution to rock and roll. Whether they are on stage by themselves, or surrounded by a 30-piece orchestra, they are what they are. Whether they're duded up in satin marching band uniforms or looking tough in leather jackets, they are always the Bee Gees.

An astute critic once said that the Bee Gees' success lay in their uncanny ability to create scenes, to create more or less fictional characters for themselves. Their sincerity when they sing is such that they can appear as jilted lovers, ambitious teenagers, defeated dreamers. They *become* their songs, so that anything they sing about is immediately transformed into a dramatic scenario. Whether they sing of a trapped miner or a Broadway bopper or an uncertain lover, they create that character, they make him real.

That's a gift few other groups can claim.

The Bee Gees were thrilled to appear in *Sgt. Pepper's Lonely Hearts Club Band* singing the Beatles' songs, because the Beatles were such a big influence on the Bee Gees' music when they were younger. The Beatles were the best, and few musicians who were learning the ropes in the mid-Sixties were unaffected by their influence on rock. Today, the Bee Gees are somewhat in the same place. The Brothers Gibb are influencing music and young musicians everywhere. Their current sounds are helping to shape the sound of rock for years to come.